George Washington Carver

Planting Ideas

Jennifer Kroll

Consultant

Glenn Manns, M.A.
Teaching American History Coordinator
Ohio Valley Educational Cooperative

Publishing Credits

Dona Herweck Rice, *Editor-in-Chief*; Lee Aucoin, *Creative Director*; Conni Medina, M.A.Ed., *Editorial Director*; Jamey Acosta, *Associate Editor;* Neri Garcia, *Senior Designer*; Stephanie Reid, *Photo Researcher*; Rachelle Cracchiolo, M.A.Ed., *Publisher*

Image Credits

cover Library of Congress; p.1 Library of Congress; p.4 Valentyn Volkov/Shutterstock; p.5 Library of Congress, LC-USZ62-136123; p.6 (left) Tony E. Walker, (right) Julie Ridge/iStockphoto; p.7 (top) Keith R. Neely, (bottom) Bruce Parrott/Shutterstock; p.8 Keith R. Neely; p.9 Benjamin Vess/Dreamstime; p.10 (left) Rozaliya/Shutterstock, (right) Ronald Sumners/Shutterstock; p.11 Keith R. Neely; p.12 The Granger Collection; p.13 National Park Service; p.14 The Granger Collection; p.15 Katrina Brown/Shutterstock; p.16 Iowa State University Library/Special Collections Department; p.17 Merritt/University of North Carolina; p.18 (left) Kurt De Bruyn/Shutterstock, (right) Joe Gough/Shutterstock; p.19 The Granger Collection; p.20 Tim Bradley; p.21 (left) Picture History/Newscom, (right) Valeev/Shutterstock; p.22 Getty Images; p.23 Bluecrayola/Shutterstock; p.24 Bettmann/Corbis; p.25 The Granger Collection; p.26 Jeffrey M. Frank/Shutterstock; p.27 Getty Imgaes; p.28 (left) Iowa State University Library/Special Collections Department, (right) Library of Congress, LC-DIG-ppmsca-05633; p.29 (left) Library of Congress, LC-USZ62-136122, (right) Getty Images

Teacher Created Materials

5301 Oceanus Drive
Huntington Beach, CA 92649-1030
http://www.tcmpub.com

ISBN 978-1-4333-1593-0
© 2011 by Teacher Created Materials, Inc.
Printed in China
Nordica.032020.CA22000192

Table of Contents

Meet George

George Washington Carver was born a slave. He grew up to be a **botanist** (BOT-n-ist). A botanist studies plants. George was also an **inventor**. An inventor makes new things. George came up with new ways to use plants. He became an **expert** on the peanut plant.

Fun Fact

Peanuts are not really nuts. They are in the same family as beans and peas.

George in his laboratory

George's Childhood

George was born in 1864. His mother was a slave. She worked for the Carver family. One night, slave robbers came to the Carvers' farm in Missouri (mi-ZOOR-ee). They took baby George and his mother. They took George's brother and sister, too.

A **model** of George's birthplace

George was born in Diamond, Missouri.

George was born during the **Civil War**. Slaves would soon be free.

Mr. Carver's friend brings George home.

Mr. Carver sent a friend to find the robbers. The friend only found baby George and his brother. He said George's mother and sister were dead. George's father had died before he was born. That meant that George and his brother were now **orphans**.

A George Washington Carver postage stamp

Fun Fact

George used the Carvers' last name. He picked his own middle name.

The Carver family raised George and his brother. Mrs. Carver taught George many things. He helped her with chores. He liked working in the garden the best. George could make anything grow. People brought sick plants to him. They called him "the plant doctor."

Fun Fact

George liked to take nature walks. He collected plants and rocks.

George as a young boy

Love of Learning

After the Civil War, slaves were free. But life was still hard for **African Americans**. The school near George's home was for white children only. The African American school was miles away. George packed a bag and started walking. He wanted to learn.

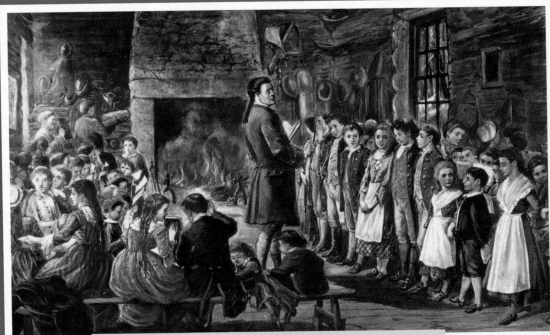

A school for white children in the 1800s

A statue of George as a young boy

An African American school in the 1800s

The African American school had one room and 75 students! George was eager to learn. Soon, he heard about a better school in another town. He moved on. As a young man, George moved often. Each time he moved, he tried to learn more.

George worked hard to pay his way. He did farm chores, cooked, and washed clothes.

George took years to finish high school. But he still wanted to learn more. Many colleges were not open to African Americans. Finally George found a college that let him study science. He studied the science of plants and farming. He was a star student.

George at the Iowa State College of Agriculture and Mechanical Arts

Fun Fact

George also studied art in college. He painted plants and flowers.

George with one of his paintings

The Peanut Man

George became a plant expert. He got a job as a college **agriculture** (AG-ri-kuhl-cher) teacher. Agriculture means farming. He was invited to work at an African American college in Alabama. George was put in charge of plants and animals at the Tuskegee (tuhs-KEE-gee) Institute.

Sometimes, George had to take care of the animals.

A peanut field

George

George in his classroom laboratory

George liked teaching college students. But he also wanted to help local farmers. Many farmers were poor. New ideas could help them. George made a school on wheels. He brought his classroom to the farmers. He showed them ways to work smarter.

George's classroom on wheels

Fun Fact

George wore old, worn suits. But he picked a flower or plant for his buttonhole each day.

George in his laboratory

George taught farmers about **crop rotation**. If they grew cotton one year and peanuts the next, the soil would be healthier. George showed them how to make many things from plants. He made 325 things from peanuts. He made peanut paint, shampoo, and even paper!

Fun Fact

George thought cars would someday use plants instead of gasoline to move.

Word got out about the "Peanut Man." During World War I, America needed more food. Leaders asked George for new ideas. He had many ideas to share. His work won awards. By the time George died at age 79, he was famous.

George met many other inventors. Henry Ford, inventor of the car, was his friend.

From left to right: Henry Ford, George, and Edsel Ford

A painting of George

A Great Man with a Great Heart

George worked hard. He loved to learn. He had a great mind, but his heart was even greater. He **improved** the lives of many people. He taught about caring for the earth. He said the earth would take care of us, too.

You can visit the George Washington Carver Museum in Tuskegee, Alabama.

George Washington Carver

1864
George Washington Carver is born in Missouri.

1894
George starts college in Iowa.

1896
George takes his job at the Tuskegee Institute.

Line

1916
During World War I, America is short on food. Leaders ask George to help.

1920s–1930s
George wins many awards.

1943
George dies at the age of 79.

Glossary

African Americans—Americans whose families first came from Africa

agriculture—the science of farming

botanist—a person who studies plants

Civil War—an American war between the northern and southern states

crop rotation—changing crops each year to keep soil healthy

expert—a person who knows a lot about one thing

improved—made something better

inventor—a person who makes something new and different

laboratory—a room where scientists work

model—a small copy of something, such as a building or airplane

orphans—children without parents

Index

Americans Today

Today, scientists like Daniel Gellar are growing peanuts, too. The peanuts will not be eaten. They will be used to make fuel. The fuel can make cars and machines go. George Washington Carver made fuel from peanuts, too. He believed we could make all we need from plants.